EXPLORING AFRICAN CIVILIZATIONS™

DISCOVERING
EGYPTIAN
DYNASTIES

THERESE SHEA

ROSEN
PUBLISHING®

New York

Published in 2014 by The Rosen Publishing Group, Inc.
29 East 21st Street, New York, NY 10010

First Edition

Library of Congress Cataloging-in-Publication Data

Shea, Therese.
Discovering Egyptian dynasties/Therese M. Shea. — First edition.
    pages cm. — (Exploring African civilizations)
ISBN 978-1-4777-1881-0 (library binding)
1. Egypt—History—To 332 B.C.—Juvenile literature. 2. Egypt—Antiquities—Juvenile literature. 3. Egypt—Civilization—To 332 B.C.—Juvenile literature. I. Title.
DT83.S535 2014
932.01—dc23

2013020101

Manufactured in the United States of America

CPSIA Compliance Information: Batch #W14YA: For further information, contact Rosen Publishing, New York, New York, at 1-800-237-9932.

A portion of the material in this book has been derived from *Egyptian Dynasties* by Joyce L. Haynes.

CONTENTS

INTRODUCTION

Egypt, in the northeast corner of Africa, is a country whose mere name inspires images of rulers long passed and riches in abundance. The recognition of Egypt as the home of one of the greatest ancient empires is well deserved. The Nile River's importance as the foundation of this civilization cannot be understated. In a land that is about 96 percent desert, this water source provided irrigation, transportation, and food, among other resources. Without the Nile, Egyptians would have been forced to live as hunter-gatherers searching for the next supply of food and water. The political, social, and artistic development that marks their history could not have occurred. Fortunately, the Nile offered them a place to settle, along the river's banks and in its valley and delta.

Egypt is often discussed geographically in terms of Upper Egypt and Lower Egypt. This stems from the Nile's flow. It travels northward from the highlands of East Africa in southern Egypt (Upper Egypt) and empties into the lower elevation of the Mediterranean Sea in the north (Lower Egypt). The peoples of Upper and Lower Egypt have always had different dialects and customs.

Scholars widely consider the Naqadah culture of Upper Egypt, which emerged about 4500 BCE, to be the most important precursor to the ancient Egyptians. (Naqadah is a town located on the west bank of the Nile, where artifacts from this period were found.) The Naqadah people lived in settlements, traded with other peoples, and mastered agriculture by around 3400 BCE. They worshipped gods later important to the

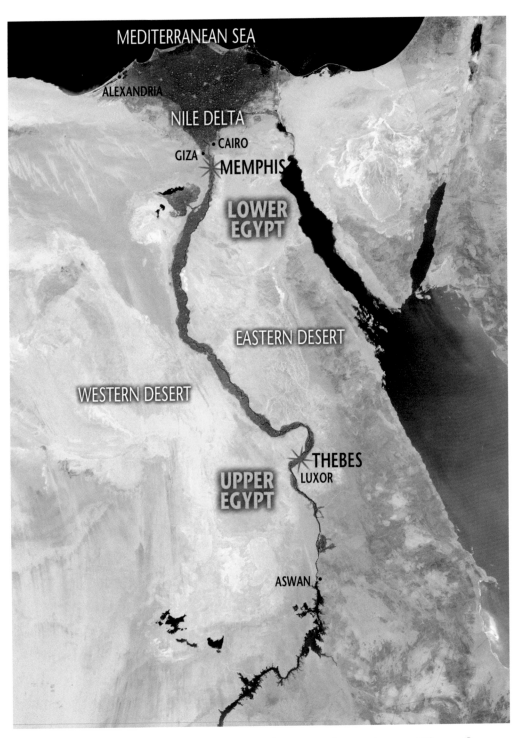

This map shows some of the ancient and modern cities of Egypt mentioned in this book. Notice their location along the Nile River.

Egyptians, including Horus, Re, and Hathor. Unlike past peoples, this culture appears to have been socially stratified, with rule by a single king. This was in contrast to the numerous ruling families who held power in Lower Egypt. The symbol of the king—the falcon—found on pottery from this period suggests that all kings came from the same family.

Around 3000 BCE, the peoples of Upper and Lower Egypt were united under a single ruler for the first time. Historians use this date as the start of ancient Egyptian civilization. Because of this unification, the king was sometimes called the "Ruler of Two Kingdoms" and "King of Upper and Lower Egypt." The king and his successors wore a pschent—a double crown, with one for each kingdom. Written records from the first dynasty list other honorific titles for the kings that convey a belief in the intermingling of the divine and the earthly in Egypt's monarchs. Kings were called the "Son of Re" (Re was the creator god and god of the sun) and the "Golden Horus" (Horus was a god in the form of a falcon and a symbol of power). This religious devotion to the Egyptian king would carry on throughout Egypt's history.

Most experts agree that thirty different dynasties ruled between 3000 and 332 BCE, when Alexander the Great conquered Egypt. For convenience, scholars divide the history of ancient Egypt into the Old Kingdom, Middle Kingdom, New Kingdom, and Late Period. Breaks between Egyptian dynasties, when a reigning family fell out of power, are called intermediate periods; these were times of conflict and rule by warring or foreign kings. For the most part, Egyptian culture was remarkably stable during the almost three thousand years it endured. However, much of it was a mystery to the modern world.

After the Macedonians, Greeks, and later the Romans conquered Egypt, Egyptian culture was altered by the influence of the Mediterranean world. Hieroglyphics, the Egyptian system of writing, fell into disuse after 394 CE, and their meaning and much of what they recorded were soon forgotten. For many centuries, nobody could read the writing on Egyptian temples and statues. Finally, in 1822, French scholar Jean-François Champollion had a breakthrough while working on an ancient inscription called the Rosetta Stone. It contained the same information in Greek, Egyptian hieroglyphics, and another form of hieroglyphics. By comparing the hieroglyphics to the Greek, Champollion decoded the ancient messages.

Since then, Egyptologists have been able to learn a great deal from unearthed hieroglyphic writings, art, and architecture. Firsthand accounts of Egyptian history and culture provide essential details about fascinating elements of this ancient culture: semi-divine pharaohs, polytheism and the afterlife, and accomplished architectural and artistic feats.

CHAPTER ONE

Pharaohs: Living Gods

The name "pharaoh" did not appear as a title for the Egyptian monarch until the 18th dynasty (1539–1292 BCE). In fact, "pharaoh" was the name of the royal palace before it became the title of the ruler himself. It originates from the Egyptian words *per* and *aa*, which together mean "great house." Today, the term encompasses all rulers of ancient Egypt.

Traditionally pharaohs were male, but occasionally a woman came to power. Pharaohs played a key role in the religious life of ancient Egypt. They were thought to be intermediaries between the gods and the living. The gods entrusted the pharaohs with the land and gave them supreme power over the people but also the responsibility to look after their needs. After each pharaoh died, he or she passed divine powers on to the next in line and became Osiris, god of the underworld and ruler of the dead. This mystique is why pharaohs commanded and inspired the building of grand monuments such as the pyramids.

Khufu and the Great Pyramid

Khufu, a pharaoh of the 4th dynasty (2575–2465 BCE), oversaw the construction of the largest pyramid in Egypt—the largest building in the world for a time. The Great Pyramid is one of three at Giza in Lower Egypt and is the only intact building of the Seven Wonders of the Ancient World.

Khufu's pyramid is about as tall as a fifty-story building and contains more than 2.3 million blocks of limestone. As soon as he became pharaoh, Khufu ordered work to begin on building the pyramid. The Great Pyramid was to be his burial place, just as other pyramids held the bodies of previous rulers. Over twenty years, thousands of men labored on it. Most of the work likely took place during the months when the Nile flooded,

Tourists in Egypt take a horseback ride around the pyramids. The Great Pyramid, the oldest and largest of the three pyramids in Giza, is seen in the background.

employing the thousands of Egyptians who normally worked in the fields. The government paid laborers with bread, beer, and other food and supplies.

The exactness of the measurements of the Great Pyramid at Giza demonstrates the advancement of mathematics in ancient Egypt. Each side of the pyramid measures about 755 feet (230 meters), with just a few inches difference on each side. Its sides rise at an angle of 51°52' and are oriented to the four points of the compass.

The exact process of pyramid building is still a mystery, even after years of study. However, there are many theories, and it most likely involved the use of simple machines. Stone blocks were probably removed carefully from quarries with pickaxes, chisels, and hammers, and then transported by sled to the pyramid site. Next, the blocks may have been dragged, possibly with rollers, up ramps constructed next to the pyramid. A block weighed up to 15 tons (14 metric tons), so this still would have been no easy feat. Levers may have aided in placing blocks at the top of the pyramids. To smooth out the sides, a layer of limestone was applied.

Pharaohs of the 18th Dynasty

Egypt's territory greatly expanded during the New Kingdom period (about 1550–1070 BCE). The empire extended east to the Euphrates River in the Middle East and south into Nubia (present-day Sudan). During this time, the remarkable Queen Hatshepsut rose to power. As the first female pharaoh, she reigned from 1473 to 1458 BCE.

Hatshepsut

When Hatshepsut's husband (and brother) Thutmose II died, the throne was left to one of Thutmose's sons, Thutmose III. Since the heir was only a child at the time, Hatshepsut officially became his regent. A few years later, she assumed the position of coruler, with all the powers of a male pharaoh. Hatshepsut is sometimes shown in Egyptian art wearing a beard, not because she disguised herself as a man, but because she had as much power as the traditional male pharaoh.

The temple of Hatshepsut at Deir el-Bahri can be found opposite the city of Luxor.

One of Hatshepsut's greatest monuments is her temple at Deir el-Bahri, built in a half-circle of cliffs on the west bank of the Nile in the ancient city of Thebes. Each of its three stories was lined with columns and placed on a separate terrace. The temple was decorated with statues of Hatshepsut as a sphinx, as a pharaoh, and as Osiris. Hieroglyphic inscriptions on the walls relate some of the female pharaoh's accomplishments, including a victorious military campaign in Nubia to the south and trading expeditions to eastern Africa.

Thutmose III

Thutmose III took the throne when he reached the ruling age in 1479 BCE, and he reigned until his death in 1426 BCE. Though he began as Hatshepsut's coruler, Egypt's power and wealth reached their highest levels under his sole kingship. Thutmose was a great military leader who took his forces into battle himself. He expanded the empire east, beyond the Sinai Peninsula, capturing ports along the eastern Mediterranean. Thutmose allowed the rulers of conquered lands to continue their reigns but as subjects of Egypt. He demanded annual tribute of valuable natural resources, such as cattle, wood, and metal. Rulers' sons were taken hostage and educated in Egypt but allowed to return to rule with a newfound appreciation and sympathy for Egyptian culture. Thutmose III's exploits are recorded on the walls of the temple at Karnak in Thebes.

As did other pharaohs, Thutmose III celebrated Egypt's strength and prosperity by building. The famous obelisks called Cleopatra's Needles were erected under Thutmose's orders at a temple to the sun god Re in Lower Egypt. Thutmose also ordered a new temple raised at Deir el-Bahri next to

Hatshepsut's. At the same time, he directed that her monuments and sculptures be destroyed, nearly erasing her from history. Many Egyptologists believe he did this to ensure that his son, Amenhotep II, would rule without regard to Hatshepsut's family line.

Akhenaton

Akhenaton, a pharaoh who ruled from 1353 to 1336 BCE, is not known for his military might but for attempting to change Egyptian religious traditions that had been observed for thousands of years. First known as Amenhotep IV, a few years into his reign he elevated Ateon, the god of the sun disk, above Amon, the king of the gods. He then tried to erase Amon's name and image from Egypt, leading to the destruction and defacement of numerous buildings and monuments. He even moved the capital of Egypt from Thebes—a city whose chief god was Amon—to a new site 200 miles (320 kilometers) north. There, he built a capital he called Akhetaton ("horizon of Aton"). The pharaoh renamed himself Akhenaton, which means "beneficial to Aton."

Akhenaton himself is thought to have instructed Egyptian artists in a new way to represent the human figure—with very long and thin heads, full hips, and narrow legs. Bodies were displayed in greater, more realistic detail. Scenes of the royal family also displayed emotion for the first time. Amarna style, as it was called, outlived many of Ahkenaton's other sweeping changes.

Once his reign was over, the Egyptians abandoned the worship of Aton, reusing limestone blocks from his temples for other construction. The site of Akhetaton at Amarna, known as

This is a sculpture of Akhenaton, the pharaoh of the 18th dynasty who introduced many changes to Egyptian culture, most of which were abandoned after his death.

Tell el-Amarna, was excavated in the twentieth century. Archaeologists unearthed hundreds of tablets of cuneiform correspondence with peoples of the Middle East, as well as busts of Akhenaton's queen Nefertiti.

Tutankhamen

Tutankhamen was Akhenaton's son and successor. First known as Tutankhaten, he came to the throne in 1333 BCE at a young age. After three years in power, he moved the capital to Memphis (near modern-day Cairo) and renamed himself Tutankhamen. He restored worship of the older gods and approved the restoration of temples.

When Tutankhamen died at age nineteen, his royal tomb had not been completed. Instead, he was buried in a small vault in the Valley of the Kings. Although thieves broke into his tomb at some point (a common occurrence), they must have been caught or frightened away; the treasures buried with the boy king were left intact. They were discovered in 1922 by British archaeologist Howard Carter. Since then, Tutankhamen's name—popularized as "King Tut"—has become world famous, less for his deeds than for his burial riches.

The few rooms of Tutankhamen's tomb contained objects most precious to the king: jewelry, clothes, weapons, and even dried foods, all ready to serve the pharaoh in the afterlife. A statue of the god Anubis, the god of mummification, protected his body. Many symbols on Tutankhamen's jewelry represent life after death, such as the scarab beetle, a symbol of rebirth, and the ankh, a hieroglyph that means "life."

Among the most impressive objects in Tutankhamen's tomb were three coffins that nested inside each other. The two

Scientists in this photo are examining the tomb of the young pharaoh Tutankhamen in the Valley of the Kings near Luxor.

outermost were made of gold-covered wood, but the innermost was solid gold. Within that lay the royal mummy, with a solid gold mask on its head. Tutankhamen's body remains in its sarcophagus in the Valley of the Kings today.

Ramses II of the 19th Dynasty

Egypt had lost some power in Asia during the rules of Akhenaton and Tutankhamen. After Tutankhamen's death, his general and chief advisor, Horemheb, ascended to the throne rather than a family member.

After Horemheb died, another military leader, Ramses I, took power in 1319 BCE, beginning the 19th dynasty. His grandson, Ramses II, reigned from about 1279 to 1213 BCE. His title—Ramses the Great—was earned through storied military exploits. His armies fought in several famous campaigns against the Hittites of the Middle East—including a battle in which Ramses did not even wear armor—and fended off the attacking forces of Libyans that threatened Egypt's borders. A period of peace and prosperity followed, during which Ramses guaranteed that his name and deeds would live on—through carved descriptions in thousands of temples all over Egypt.

In southern Egypt at Abu Simbel, Ramses II oversaw the building of two temples carved into the sandstone cliffs. Four colossal seated statues of the pharaoh, each 66 feet (20 m) tall, still guard the entrance outside. Around the bottom of the statues are small figures representing Ramses's children (of which he may have had one hundred); his beloved queen Nefertari; and his mother, Muttuy. Many pharaohs called themselves Ramses after him, but none ever matched his feats. His death marked the beginning of a period of turmoil and an overall weakening of Egypt's empire.

Foreign Rule

Alexander the Great of Macedonia, an ancient kingdom in northern Greece, conquered Egypt in 332 BCE, as he had much of the Mediterranean world. He founded and named Alexandria, the great coastal city in Egypt. After Alexander's death in 323 BCE, one of Alexander's trusted generals, Ptolemy I Soter, became satrap (governor) of Egypt. Ptolemy reigned from 323

TUT'S DEMISE

Why did Tutankhamen die so young? Among the many theorized diagnoses are malaria and degenerative bone disease. One of the most recent theories came in 2012. Dr. Hutan Ashrafian told ABC News that Tut's remains show signs that the young pharaoh had temporal lobe epilepsy. His relatives appear to have had the same affliction. Whatever ailment Tutankhamen suffered, royal physicians could not cure it.

In ancient Egypt, sickness and disease were often treated first by priests with prayers to a certain god or with incantations thought to have magical qualities. However, ancient Egyptian doctors did understand certain mainstays of health such as the importance of hygiene. There were even surgeries to reset bones as early as 2750 BCE.

to 285 BCE. He mixed the Greek and Egyptian religious traditions and founded the famous library at Alexandria. Ptolemy became so well accepted by the native people that he was named a god after his death, just like true Egyptian pharaohs of past dynasties.

For the next 250 years, rulers of the Ptolemaic line controlled Egypt. Fifteen pharaohs named Ptolemy reigned during that period. Later in the dynasty, members of the royal family plotted against relatives who stood between them and the throne. Murders were frequent.

The famous queen Cleopatra was the seventh pharaoh of that name. When Cleopatra VII took the throne at age eighteen in 51 BCE, along with her brother, Egypt and the Roman Empire were the two great powers in the Mediterranean. In 48 BCE, Julius Caesar arrived in Alexandria, then the capital, and was charmed by the young queen. Seeking absolute power over the Mediterranean world, these two rulers allied their forces, assuring that Cleopatra kept the throne.

After Julius Caesar was assassinated in Rome in 44 BCE, his heir, Octavian, and one of his generals, Mark Antony, vied for control. Cleopatra sided with Mark Antony. In 31 BCE, Octavian defeated Antony and Cleopatra at the Battle of Actium. Antony committed suicide after receiving false news of Cleopatra's death. Then Cleopatra, too, killed herself. This ushered in the Roman rule of Egypt.

Cleopatra was not a great builder as many of her predecessors had been. The one temple she was building at the time of her death was the Temple of Hathor. Her likeness is carved into its walls. Her face is found on coins as well. Tales of Cleopatra's beauty have been passed down through history, but her cunning and strength as a ruler in the dying days of the Ptolemaic dynasty are impossible to deny.

CHAPTER TWO

Religion and the Afterlife

The tombs, monuments, temples, and written accounts of the pharaohs reveal much about the religious beliefs and practices of the ancient Egyptians. Religion was a guiding force in many aspects of Egyptian daily life. It helped people make sense of the human body, and understand the natural world. It also gave them hope for an afterlife.

Preparing for the Afterlife

Egyptians believed every person had a vital life force, somewhat like a soul. The part of the soul called the *ka* did not perish with the human body. Offerings in a tomb of food, drink, and riches were for the *ka*, which was eternally youthful. Another part of the soul that lived on was the *ba*. The *ba* was believed to journey away from the dead body, unlike the *ka*, but always returned. A person's immortal life was endangered if anything happened to the body. This was why mummification, the preservation of the body, was considered necessary.

Mummification

Mummification was an embalming process that prevented the decay of a corpse. Though the Egyptians were not the only

These canopic jars contain embalmed organs. The lids of the jars represent the four sons of the god Horus.

culture to practice it, they perfected their method. The stomach, liver, intestines, and lungs were removed and placed in special containers called canopic jars. (In later periods, the organs were placed back in the body.) The brain was discarded after removing it from the skull with a long, thin hook. The heart remained. The body was packed and surrounded with a blend of salts called natron. Natron sucked the moisture out of the body after about forty days.

When the body was dry and leathery, it was packed with wood shavings and spices, covered with oils, and wrapped in linen bandages. Amulets between layers were meant to

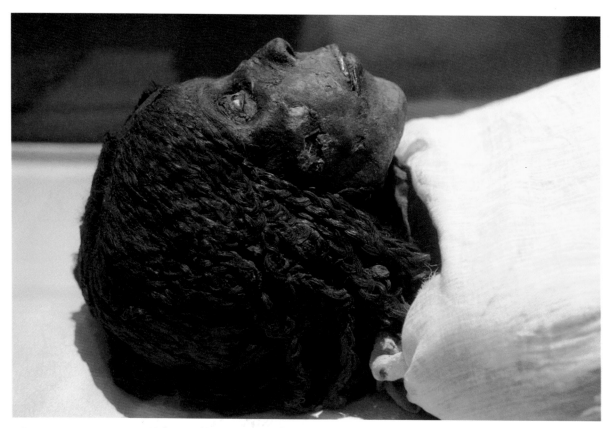

This is the mummy of Nodjmet, wife of high priest Herihor (1080–945 BCE) and possibly sister to Ramses XI.

protect the body on its journey. Resin, which turned as dark as tar, helped seal the linen bandages. (The word "mummy" comes from the Arabic word *mumia*, which means "tar.") Cloth was wrapped around the mummy. Finally the body was placed in a coffin (or coffins) and laid in a stone sarcophagus.

Opening of the Mouth Ceremony

Egyptians believed that mummification immobilized the spirit of the dead person. Before placing the mummy in the tomb,

THE ROLES OF EGYPTIAN PRIESTS

Daily worship in Egypt's temples was based on the belief that the spirit of the god roamed the earth. At dawn, the high priest broke the clay seal on the door of the shrine that held the god's statue. The god was reawakened by a priest's incantations and offered food and drink. After a specified amount of time had passed, the priests removed what the god had not spiritually "eaten" (and probably ate the food themselves). The statue was cleaned, perfumed, and dressed in new linens. This ritual was repeated twice a day, and then at night a new clay seal was applied to the door.

Other priests acted as astronomers and astrologers. They observed natural phenomena and determined when religious holidays and festivals should start. They predicted which days were lucky, neutral, or unlucky. Other priests were timekeepers, tending the great granite water clocks that kept time through the night when the sun's position could not be measured. The Egyptian calendar had weeks of ten days each, and three weeks equaled a month. Egyptian astronomers calculated a surprisingly accurate solar calendar based on a year of 365.25 days. The exact measurement of a year is 365.242199 days.

priests performed the "Opening of the Mouth" ceremony to release the *ka* and *ba*. The mummy was held upright while the chief priest burned incense and poured offerings. The priest touched the mummy's mouth and eyes with a special instrument, symbolically opening them and allowing the spirit to receive offerings of food and drink. As the priests performed the ceremony, they recited: "You live again, you revive always, you have become young again, you are young again and forever." The ceremony was also performed on statues, which were believed to have the ability to house the *ka*.

The Scales of Maat

The ancient Egyptians thought their good and bad deeds were evaluated after death in a ceremony overseen by the god Osiris. Egyptians believed that all of their actions were recorded in the heart. After death, the heart was placed on one side of a great scale and weighed against a sacred ostrich feather. The feather represented Maat, the goddess of truth, order, and justice. If the heart was heavier than the feather, it was weighed down by bad deeds. They believed the heart would then be thrown into a lake of fire or eaten by a beast monster named Am-mut, whose name means "devourer of the dead." There was no afterlife for the

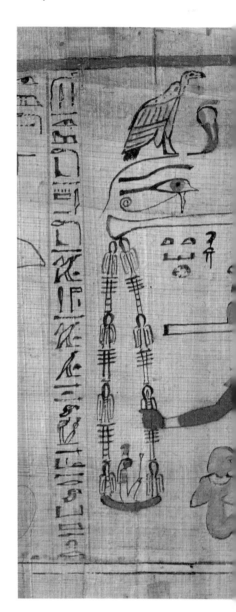

guilty. If the heart balanced with the feather, the deceased was pronounced "true of voice" and led into the heavenly realm to enjoy eternal life. The specifics of the ceremony were included in a funereal text called the *Book of the Dead*.

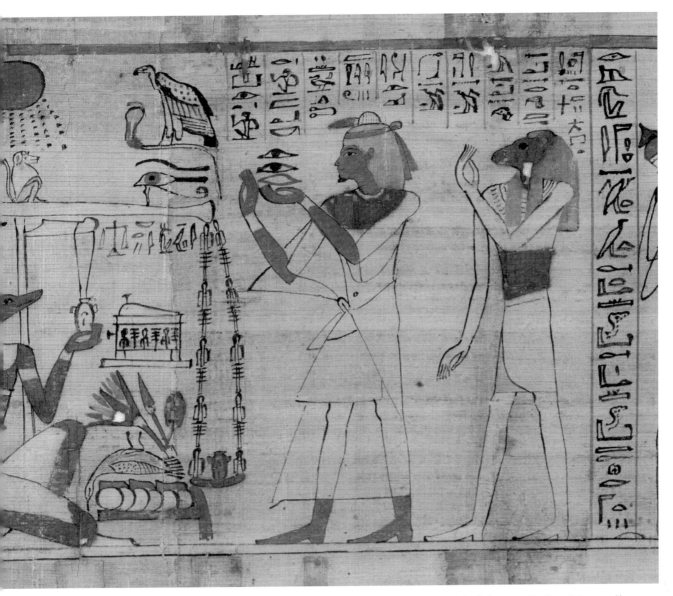

This image from the *Book of the Dead* shows the "Weighing of the Heart" ceremony. The afterlife hangs in the balance for the deceased.

Gods

The polytheistic ancient Egyptians worshipped many gods and goddesses, who were represented in art as partly or completely human or animal. Egypt was divided into districts, each with its own god, traditions, and customs. Some gods were only honored locally, whereas others were revered nationally. Sometimes gods were "promoted." When a major Egyptian city was named the capital city, its local god was worshipped nationally. During the Old Kingdom, the capital was Memphis, and the local god Ptah, the god of craftsmen, became important throughout the country. Similarly, in the New Kingdom, when Thebes was the capital, temples and shrines to Amon were erected everywhere: Amon became the god of the pharaoh and of the whole Egyptian empire. Just as the pharaoh Akhenaton attempted to promote the god Aton to supreme importance, a pharaoh often decided which gods were of the most importance.

Nine gods play key roles in the Egyptian creation myth. The sun god, Re, arose on a hill in the middle of the ocean of chaos. He created a pair of deities by spitting: Shu, god of air, and Tefnut, goddess of moisture. Shu and Tefnut produced two children: Geb, god of earth, and Nut, the sky goddess. They, in turn, had four children named Osiris, Isis, Seth, and Nepthys.

Many versions of the myth of Isis and Osiris exist. Most stories include the following details: Osiris became the first king and took Isis as his wife. Their evil brother Seth murdered Osiris. However, Osiris was resurrected for a time, and Isis had

These figurines displayed in the Louvre museum in Paris, France, represent the Egyptian gods Horus (*left*), Osiris (*middle*), and Isis (*right*).

a child, Horus. Horus took the form of a falcon whose eyes were the sun and moon. In a terrible battle with Seth, Horus's left eye was damaged (representing the phases of the moon), but Horus eventually killed his father's murderer. Horus became king on earth and the god of the sky, and Osiris was honored as the god of the underworld.

Everyone who took the throne of Egypt was compared to the good and triumphant king Horus and was even called "The Horus" or the "Golden Horus." When pharaohs died, they were called "The Osiris" and presumed to live eternally like the god.

Housing the Gods

Egyptian temples were either built to honor a god (cult temples) or house the bodies and treasures of dead pharaohs (mortuary temples). In cult temples, Egyptians believed the spirit of the god could enter a statue housed in the sacred sanctuary at the back of the temple. Usually only priests and royalty had access to this area. Commoners could not even enter the temple, except during religious festivals; they usually worshipped outside the walls and at household shrines.

A temple complex consisted of many structures, including dwellings for priests and buildings ranging from slaughter-houses to grain storage houses. The temple was a center of both religious and economic activity. During the reign of Ramses III, the temple of Amon at Karnak had 433 orchards, about 421,000 head of livestock, 65 villages, 46 workshops and buildings, and a total labor force of more than 81,000.

The Temple of Luxor in Thebes was dedicated to the worship of Amon, believed to be the king of the gods and the god of the pharaohs. Two statues of the pharaoh Ramses II guard the temple's entrance.

In many major temples, a building called the "House of Life" served as a center for scholarly thought and writings. Here, scribes copied religious, medical, and technical documents, though few of these scrolls have survived. Many famous Greek philosophers spent time at Egyptian temples, including Plato, who studied geometry and religion in Egypt for thirteen years.

CHAPTER THREE

The Arts of Ancient Egypt

Writing, painting, drawing, and sculpture were important in ancient Egypt. These arts have opened the door to our understanding of the ancient culture. Egyptians made the earliest form of paper from the papyrus plant that grew along the Nile River. Strips of the plant were pounded together, dried, and polished to smooth its surface and prepare it for writing. Reeds were made into writing instruments, and a soot and beeswax mixture served as black ink. Different minerals could be mixed in to make colored inks as well.

Writing

Egyptian hieroglyphic writing dates from around 3000 BCE. The word "hieroglyph" is a Greek word meaning "sacred carving." The Egyptians' own name for their writing was *mdju netjer*, or "words of the gods," and hieroglyphs were used mostly on monuments, temples, tombs, and religious writings.

The ancient Egyptians who learned to read and write were called scribes, and they were trained in their craft in special schools. A scribe was most likely from a middle-class family

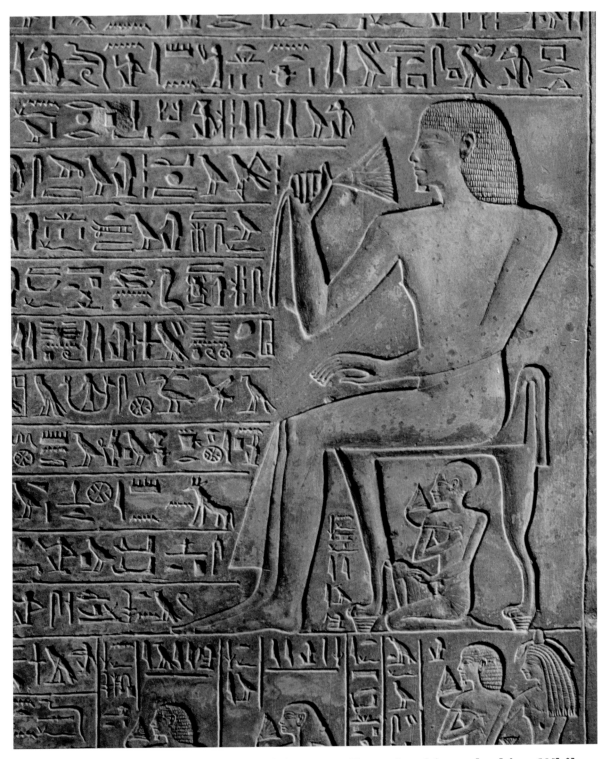

One of the earliest systems of writing was Egyptian hieroglyphics. While some of these symbols stand for single sounds, others stand for two or three sounds, or even whole words.

that could afford the luxury of sending a child to school. Scribes learned more than seven hundred signs. Each was a picture of an object, animal, or person. But hieroglyphs were not simply picture writing. Some signs represented a sound or combination of sounds. Others were visual aids—for example, a picture of legs to illustrate the word "run." There were hieroglyphs for numbers as well: a rope hieroglyph translated into one hundred, a lotus flower was one thousand, and one million was a god with his hands in the air. Hieroglyphs were written right to left, left to right, and top to bottom. They were generally read according to the orientation of the faces of the humans or animals in the signs.

A form of writing called hieratic script was developed around the same time as hieroglyphics. It was a simplified form of pictorial writing commonly used for business, religious, and legal documents. The differences between hieratic and hieroglyphic writing can be compared to the differences between cursive and printed writing. Hieratic script was used on papyrus and rarely found on stone.

Around 660 BCE, demotic writing arose. "Demotic" is Greek for "popular writing," and it was used for stories, poems, and business purposes. Egyptians called it *sekh shat*, meaning "writing for documents." Demotic writing was later replaced by the Greek alphabet, when Egypt fell under Greek rule. Greek, demotic, and hieroglyphic writing were all found on a stone discovered in 1799 near the town of Rosetta, about 35 miles (56 km) northeast of Alexandria. The Rosetta Stone became the key to understanding Egyptian hieroglyphic writing.

THE RHIND PAPYRUS

A papyrus scroll dating back to 1650 BCE provides information about Egyptian concepts in mathematics. Called the Rhind papyrus, it is written in hieratic script and shows calculations for a pyramid as well as other math problems. For example, a cubit was an Egyptian unit of measurement based on the length of an arm from the elbow to the tip of the middle finger. The scroll explains that one cubit equaled seven "palms."

The problems on the Rhind papyrus show that pyramids were carefully calculated. However, as impressive as many of the surviving pyramids are today, some earlier pyramids had flaws that led to their collapse. The engineers incorrectly calculated how stressful conditions would affect each pyramid's sides. This was the case with the pyramid of Medum, found near Memphis on the west bank of the Nile River. Scholars believe that the pyramid was constructed at the order of the pharaoh Huni of the 3rd dynasty, who ruled from 2650 to about 2575 BCE. The structure was originally a stepped pyramid, built in the style of the ziggurat temples of an earlier Mesopotamian culture. Its eight steps were then smoothed and filled in to turn it into a true pyramid. However, at some point, the sides collapsed. The debris surrounds the pyramid of Medum to this day.

Egyptian Art

Art adorning Egyptian tombs was more than mere decoration. Egyptians believed the images would come alive in the after-life. For this reason, no matter what age they died, the dead are shown as young and attractive, in beautiful settings or enjoying banquets. Sometimes they are pictured being entertained by groups of musicians playing the harp, lyre, lute, and flute. (No musical notes were ever written down, so no one is sure what ancient Egyptian music sounded like.) Dancers accompanied them, playing tambourines and clappers like castanets and sometimes even performing acrobatics. Scenes such as this suggested a celebratory afterlife for the dead.

In most Egyptian drawing, every body part is displayed from its most distinctive point of view. A face was shown from the side to reveal its profile, but the eye was drawn facing the front. Shoulders were drawn from the front, but the legs from the side. These combinations of views are what make Egyptian art unique and lifelike, although not true to nature.

Similarly, Egyptian artists did not draw closer objects larger and farther ones smaller to show perspective. They made the more important people, gods, and objects larger than the less important. A servant, for example, would be drawn half the size of his or her master or mistress, whereas pharaohs and gods were depicted as the same size because their stature was similar in society.

Artists often worked together to create a scene. A mural, for example, would be made in a sequence of steps. First, an artist would draw guidelines in red ink. Then black ink was used for

This mural found in Thebes depicts a prince and his wife in typical Egyptian artistic style. The figures' torsos are facing the viewer, though their heads and legs are shown from the side.

correction. Next, tempera paint filled in the scene. Murals were often the artwork of choice on mud or poor-quality stone. Reliefs were carved on stone of good quality and sometimes painted.

Sculpture was typically created for funerary and religious purposes. Statues display Hatshepsut and Thutmose III in regal poses, while massive structures represent Ramses II and Amenhotep III. Nonroyal figures were sometimes used as votive statues in temples, forever offering gods supplication and prayers. Sculptures, even ones that were intricately carved, were used as surfaces for religious text as well.

The art of ancient Egypt has allowed the civilization's legacy to live on. In a way, it has made the ancient culture immortal, still celebrated years after its collapse.

CHAPTER FOUR

Life on the Nile

A great deal of focus in the study of ancient Egypt is devoted to the lives of the pharaohs. But thousands of objects, pieces of artwork, and writings from that time inform Egyptologists about the lives of common Egyptians. Where they lived, what they looked like, what they ate, and how they spent their time are some of the questions that can now be answered. Without a doubt, the Nile was the source and center of life for most ancient Egyptians.

Farming and Food

Ancient Egyptians mastered the skills of agriculture. Agriculture was introduced to the Egyptians around the fifth millennium BCE. Archaeologists suspect that some of the crops, and the knowledge of their cultivation, came from the Middle East.

Egyptian farming depended on the flooding of the Nile River each summer. When the floodwaters receded, they left a rich deposit of silt along the banks of the river. Farmers then worked the land, plowing by hand or with oxen, and seeded the soil. Man-made canals carried water inland and provided irrigation for the growing harvest; basins were also dug and used to trap water. Lever-like devices called shadufs lifted the water in buckets or skins from the basins. Months later, an abundant yield provided most of the food needed to feed the people of Egypt.

So important was the annual flooding of the Nile that the year was divided into three seasons. *Akhet*, which means "inundation," was from June to September, when the land was flooded with the Nile's waters. During this time, farmers

A fresco found in a tomb shows an Egyptian peasant farmer using a shaduf, a device using a weight and a lever to lift water needed for irrigation.

worked on the pyramids or other construction projects and readied their tools for farming. *Peret* means "growing." Extending from October to February, this was the time of year when the floodwaters left and seeds could be sown into the fertile ground. *Shemu*, from March to May, was the harvest season. Men, women, and children flocked to the fields with sickles and baskets to bring in the crops. Flooding was imprecise and unpredictable, though. Too much rainfall or drought sometimes meant a poor harvest or famine.

The most important crops were barley and wheat. From this yield came bread and beer—the two staples of the Egyptian diet. Vegetables eaten in Egypt included onions, garlic, leeks, cucumbers, lentils, and lettuce. Fruits included dates, figs, pomegranates, and grapes. The average family ate mostly fish for protein because it was readily available in the Nile. Wealthier Egyptians regularly feasted on meat from oxen, gazelles, antelope, goats, ducks, and geese. For dessert, they ate cakes in spiral, animal, or human shapes, which were flavored with honey, sesame, or dates.

Food and wine were stored in pottery. Oils were placed in vessels with small necks made for pouring, and grains and flours were stored in larger jars. Fish and meat were dried, salted, and placed in jars, which were sealed to preserve their contents. Food did not last long in the hot climate, though some houses had an underground compartment for cooler storage.

Shelter

Stone was difficult to remove from the desert, so it was only used for important temples and buildings. Most ancient

EGYPT'S SUPERHIGHWAY

While Egypt was self-sufficient in food for the most part, trade with neighboring regions was important for other reasons. Since Egypt was a desert nation, trees were scarce. Wood had to be imported from other countries. Gold and ivory were brought in from Nubia in the south. Meanwhile, Egypt exported products such as linen, papyrus, and various grains.

The flow of the Nile in Egypt made it the superhighway of travel and facilitated trade. The cool breezes on the river and the view of the lush green marshes on either side of the Nile made river travel far more pleasant than walking along the desert paths or bumping along on the back of a donkey. Goods and people journeyed on rafts made of reeds that grew along the Nile. Sturdier wooden sailboats called feluccas were used for longer trading expeditions. The current of the Nile and a little rowing easily carried vessels northward. To travel south, it was necessary to raise a sail to catch the wind. Cataracts—rocky sections of shallowness—prohibited travel as far as equatorial Africa, however.

Egyptians—like many Egyptians today—lived in houses made of mud bricks. Bricks were made by packing a mixture of straw and mud from the banks of the Nile into rectangular wooden molds, which were left in the sun to dry. Homes had flat roofs supported by palm tree trunks. Poor Egyptians had one- or two-room huts, but some homes in cities had as many as three stories. Wealthier Egyptians in the country had estates of more than fifty rooms surrounded by luxurious gardens and pools.

The hot weather dictated the design of homes. Windows were small and high, keeping out the sun, dust, and sand. Walls were coated with white plaster, and the floors were covered with reed mats, which could be wet to cool the house. Many houses had stairs going up to a rooftop terrace, where the family could sit at night or even sleep if the interior of the home was too warm.

Common households had only reed stools as furniture and mats on the floor as beds. Wealthier families owned fine wooden chairs, and some had wooden beds with leather mattresses. A wooden headrest, rather than a padded pillow, was used for sleeping. Instead of cupboards and bureaus, Egyptians used small wooden chests and covered baskets. Lamps were bowls filled with oil; a wick was lit to provide light.

Egyptian Beauty and Fashion

All classes of ancient Egyptians were markedly concerned with personal cleanliness and appearance. Natron, the sodium compound found in the Nile's waters, was used to make toothpaste. Other materials, such as body oils, scents, and certain cosmetics, were imported. Both Egyptian men and women rubbed scented oils on their skin to combat the hot, dusty climate. Both also outlined their eyes with makeup made of ground minerals such as kohl, attempting to make the eyes

This is a bust of a young woman who was possibly a daughter of Akhenaton or a princess in the court of Tutankhamen. She wears her hair in a side lock, a braided lock of hair popular for youths.

look larger. Rouge was used on cheeks, red ointment on lips, and white powders on skin to smooth the complexion.

Egyptians spent a lot of time on their hair, as demonstrated by the many wigs, braids, hair curlers, and hairpins that have been found in tombs. Hairstylists are featured on frescoes, urns, and coffins. Hair fashions changed rapidly, especially during the New Kingdom.

Egyptians wore linen clothing. Linen was made from flax, a plant that grew along the Nile. Most clothing was uncolored, though people adorned themselves with vibrant jewelry and beads, especially in the form of bands or collars around the neck and shoulders. Footwear was made out of papyrus, leather, or palm leaves.

During the Old Kingdom, men wore short, simple skirts tied or belted at the waist. A cape partly covered their bare upper half. Women typically dressed in ankle-length sheath gowns. Common laborers and children often wore only loincloths or nothing at all, practical attire for the hot climate. By the New Kingdom, fashions had become more elaborate and complicated for both men and women of the royalty and priesthood, and royal children were dressed much like their parents.

Tutankhamen's tomb held tunics, shirts, skirts, sashes, socks, headdresses, scarves, and gloves. Similarly, cosmetics, mirrors, tweezers, combs, and razors have been found in graves. All signify the importance of beauty and fashion in Egyptian life, as well as in the afterlife.

CHAPTER FIVE

Egyptians Today

People from all over the world visit Egypt hoping to catch a glimpse into its rich past. The pyramids stand as enormous reminders of the ancient civilization that existed. Remnants of the ancient culture survive in the mud-brick homes and shadufs of many Egyptian farmers today. But Egypt is not a mausoleum of artifacts. The Arab Republic of Egypt, as it is now called, is a vibrant and modern country.

As in the past, most Egyptians reside near the country's water supply. In fact, according to the U.S. Department of State, 99 percent of Egypt's citizens live near the Nile River and the Suez Canal, the man-made waterway connecting the Mediterranean Sea and the Red Sea. Most of these people live in bustling, contemporary cities such as Alexandria, Cairo, Luxor, Aswan, and Port Said. In modern settings, young people, while desiring to better their situation politically and economically, often feel the pull of their parents' traditions.

Many Cultures

Ethnic Egyptians—a mixture of African and Arab ancestry—are the majority in the Nile valley and delta, but Egypt is home to a multicultural society. Ethnic minorities include Arabs, Turks,

Traffic courses through Tahrir Square in Cairo, Egypt's capital city. Cairo is a modern city, the largest in Africa.

and Greeks. They also include the Nubians of southern Egypt, Berbers of the Siwa Oasis in northwest Egypt, Bedouins of the western and eastern deserts and the Sinai Peninsula, and tribal peoples such as the Beja and Dom. Some live as nomads similarly to their ancestors, traveling with animals in search of water and grazing land. However, modernization has touched all parts of life. For example, even those who wear the traditional dress of days past may watch television and use cell phones.

The official language of Egypt is Arabic, but many other languages are spoken and understood, especially French and

English. Islam is the official religion, and about 90 percent of Egyptians claim to be Muslims, according to the U.S. Central Intelligence Agency's (CIA) online *World Factbook*. Most non-Muslims are Christians.

Egyptians enjoy sports, especially soccer (called football). Art, music, and dancing are other sources of entertainment. Different regions of the country are known for certain traditional styles of dancing. The people of the Sinai Peninsula may wear hand-embroidered clothing while performing sword

Egyptians raise their national flag for their team at a World Cup soccer game. Egypt is one of the most competitive African teams, and it is only the second Arab nation to make the top ten in the FIFA world rankings.

dances. Traditional instruments such as the stringed *simsimiyya*, which is somewhat like a lyre or harp, is played to accompany dancers of *bambutiyya*, especially in Port Said. The Nubians of southern Egypt are known for their colorful costumes and joyful dances. Egypt also has a thriving film and television industry, though its products are more familiar to the Middle East than to the Western world.

ASWAN HIGH DAM

It took an impressive structure to tame the floods of the Nile River. The Aswan High Dam (*Saad el Aali* in Arabic) is 364 feet (111 m) high, 12,562 feet (3,833 m) long, and cost about $1 billion to construct. It provides regular irrigation for Egypt's farmland. Egyptian farmers no longer have to wonder, as their ancestors did, whether the floods will come, if too much water will arrive, or if they will struggle through drought or famine. The dam also provides a great amount of hydroelectric power. However, the structure has drawbacks as well. Much of the silt that the floods once carried inland—the silt that made the land so fertile—is caught in the Lake Nasser reservoir and in canals. To make up for the millions of tons of silt once deposited by the Nile, artificial fertilizers are used, though they are less effective.

The Economy

Unsurprisingly, most of Egypt's economic activity is centered in the cities and towns of the Nile River valley. About one-third of the nation's labor force works in agriculture, according to the CIA's *World Factbook*. Profitable goods include cotton, rice, corn, wheat, beans, fruits, vegetables, cattle, water buffalo, sheep, and goats. The Nile provides about 190 varieties of fish as well.

The construction of the Aswan High Dam on the Nile changed the lives of farmers forever. Since its completion in 1970, the water that once flooded the banks of the Nile each year is stored and controlled by this dam, allowing for perennial irrigation. The dam also created Lake Nasser, now used for fishing and tourism.

Egyptians have environmental concerns that must be addressed to protect their agricultural economy. Expanding urban centers are encroaching on farmland. Chemical pesticides used on farmland pollute the water, harming fish, coral, and other marine life. Pollution from cities endangers both the soil and water supplies.

Tourist Destinations

The remainder of the Egyptian economy centers on industry—textiles, chemicals, pharmaceuticals, and construction—and services, most notably tourism. People are attracted to the region's history and travel from all over the world to see its monuments and treasures from the past. Since most of Egypt

A TIME OF UNREST

There is much poverty in modern Egypt, a condition that has led to political unrest and calls for economic reform. According to the CIA's *World Factbook,* about 20 percent of the population of more than eighty-three million lives in poverty, and many of these are peasant farmers who raise vital crops for the country.

In 2011, a force rose up to overthrow president Hosni Mubarak, clamoring against the injustice and corruption of his government. Mubarak stepped down after thirty years in power. Egypt's military ruled until elections were held in 2012, after which Mohammed Morsi became the fifth president of Egypt. Under Morsi, a new, controversial constitution was drafted and approved, but in 2013, the Egyptian military ousted Morsi and the constitution was suspended. Violence erupted while the country awaited elections.

Egypt's valuable tourist industry has been hit hard by the political unrest. According to an article in the *Economist,* in 2010, a record fourteen million travelers chose Egypt as their destination. However, following the ousting of Mubarak, 4.5 million fewer tourists ventured into the country. The numbers still haven't recovered to their typical levels. Those who rely on tourism for their livelihoods—including guides, hotel workers, and business and restaurant owners—are hoping a period of peace and security will lure more tourists back to Egypt's ancient treasures in the near future.

is desert, fall and spring are the optimal times for tourists hoping to avoid the heat. Many choose to travel down the Nile by boat during the mild Egyptian winter. Resorts along the shore of the Red Sea are also popular.

Besides the pyramids of Giza outside of Cairo, there are other inspiring landmarks for tourists to see today. The Great Sphinx, with the body of a lion and the head of a man, guards the pyramid of Khafre, a king of the 4th dynasty who ruled from about 2520 to 2494 BCE. In the city of Luxor, near the Nile River, a beautiful temple built around 1400 BCE stands among

Tourists in Egypt visit the Great Sphinx at Giza. The Sphinx is the largest monolith statue in the world, which means it is made of a single block of stone. Khafre's pyramid tomb can be seen to the left.

the modern buildings. Built by Amenhotep III and Ramses II, the temple was an enormous construction dedicated to several gods, including Ka.

Nearby, the ancient city of Thebes lives on in the ruins of Karnak, its temple district. About thirty pharaohs oversaw the building of the temples, statues, and sacred pool there. In the center lies Hypostyle Hall, which is surrounded by over one hundred columns. The Valley of the Kings also lies near Luxor. Besides Tutankhamen's mummy, more than sixty other tombs can be found there.

The Egyptian Museum of Antiquities houses as many as 120,000 ancient Egyptian artifacts, more than any museum in the world. Located in Cairo, the museum showcases objects from Tutankhamen's tomb and twenty-seven mummies. Ancient games, furniture, weapons, dishes, and other objects are also on display.

The Library of Alexandria, founded in the third century BCE by Ptolemy I, was the largest library of its time. It was the center of learning for centuries and at one point contained more than seven hundred thousand scrolls. Euclid outlined the first principles of geometry there, and Julius Caesar designed the Julian calendar within its walls. Though the original library was destroyed in the third century CE, a new one was built near its ruins.

In southern Egypt, the impressive site of Abu Simbel attracts people to the shores of Lake Nasser. The temple complex, guarded by four statues of Ramses II, had stood on the west bank of the Nile since the thirteenth century BCE. However, after the construction of the Aswan High Dam, Abu Simbel was threatened by the waters of the river that created Lake Nasser. It was successfully moved a short distance to safety.

Though not as ancient as many of Egypt's most revered monuments, the marketplace called the Khan al-Kahlili Bazaar dates back to 1382. It was established as a trading post for spices in Cairo, which is now a city of ten million people. Today's shoppers find much more, including gems, fabrics, silver, herbs, and tea.

The ancient and modern worlds collide in Egypt. The fifth century BCE Greek historian Herodotus called Egypt the "gift of the Nile." Undoubtedly, the ancient treasures, monuments, writings, and culture of the Egyptian civilization will continue to delight and amaze for generations to come.

c. 4500 BCE Naqadah culture begins in Upper Egypt.

c. 3500 BCE The Naqadah people master agriculture.

c. 3000 BCE Upper and Lower Egypt are united under a single ruler. The earliest evidence of hieroglyphic writing dates to this time.

c. 2650–c. 2575 BCE Huni constructs the pyramid at Medum.

c. 2575 BCE The Old Kingdom begins.

c. 2551–c. 2528 BCE Khufu reigns and builds the Great Pyramid at Giza.

c. 2520– c. 2494 BCE Khafre rules and builds the Great Sphinx.

1938 BCE The Middle Kingdom begins.

c. 1650 BCE The Rhind papyrus, which included calculations for pyramid building, is written.

c. 1539 BCE The New Kingdom begins.

1473–1458 BCE Hatshepsut rules as the first female pharaoh.

1458–1426 BCE Thutmose III becomes sole ruler; Egypt's power and wealth reach their highest levels.

c. 1400 BCE The Temple of Luxor is constructed.

1353 to 1336 BCE Akhenaton attempts to change Egyptian religious traditions.

1333–1323 BCE Tutankhamen restores old gods.

1319 BCE Ramses I takes power and begins the 19th dynasty.

1279 to 1213 BCE Ramses II, the great military ruler, reigns.

664 BCE The Late Period begins.

c. 660 BCE Demotic writing arises.

332 BCE Alexander the Great of Macedonia conquers Egypt.

323 BCE Greek rule begins under Ptolemy I Soter, who mixes Greek and Egyptian cultures.

c. 300 BCE The Library of Alexandria, the largest library of its time, is built.

51–30 BCE Cleopatra VII begins her rule.

48 BCE Julius Caesar joins forces with Cleopatra.

31 BCE Antony and Cleopatra are defeated by Octavian at the Battle of Actium.

30 BCE Roman rule of Egypt begins.

cuneiform A form of writing that uses wedge-shaped characters.

delta A triangular or fan-shaped piece of land made by mud and sand that collects at the mouth of a river.

dialect A form of a language that is spoken only in a certain area.

dynasty A line of rulers who belong to the same family.

Egyptologist An archaeologist who specializes in the culture and artifacts of ancient Egyptian civilization.

embalm To treat a dead body with a substance to preserve it from decay.

fresco A painting on a surface made by brushing watercolors onto wet or damp plaster.

incantation The chanting or uttering of words designed to produce a particular effect.

inundation The state of covering with a flood; deluge.

jackal A wild mammal that resembles a dog.

malaria A human disease caused by parasites in the red blood cells, transmitted by the bite of mosquitoes. It is characterized by periodic attacks of chills and fever.

oasis A fertile area in a desert where plants grow and travelers can get water supplies.

obelisk A four-sided pillar of stone that becomes narrower as it rises and has a top shaped like a pyramid.

oust To use force to remove someone from a place or position.

perennial Constantly recurring.

polytheism Worship of or belief in more than one god.

precursor A person or thing that precedes; predecessor.

regent A person who rules on behalf of a monarch who is unable to rule because of youth, illness, or absence.

relief Shallow carving on a flat stone surface.

sarcophagus An ancient stone or marble coffin, often decorated with sculpture and inscriptions.

silt Fine-grained sediment at the bottom of a river.

sphinx In Egyptian mythology, a creature with a lion's body and the head of a man, ram, or bird.

stratified Having a hierarchy of social classes.

tempera A technique of painting with colors made from pigments mixed with water and another substance.

tribute A payment made by one ruler or state to another as a sign of obedience.

votive offering Something offered, given, or dedicated to the gods in gratitude or to encourage their favor.

FOR MORE INFORMATION

American Research Center in Egypt (ARCE)
1256 Briarcliff Road NE
Building A, Suite 423W
Atlanta, GA 30306
(404) 712 9854
Web site: http://www.arce.org
ARCE is an organization that supports archaeology, research, and conservation efforts in Egypt. Find videos and more on its Web site.

Canadian Museum of Civilization
100 Laurier Street
Gatineau, QC K1A 0M8
Canada
(800) 555 5621
Web site: http://www.civilization.ca
This museum's Mysteries of Egypt exhibit and Web site highlight the artifacts of pharaohs Hatshepsut and Tutankhamen.

The Field Museum
1400 S. Lake Shore Drive
Chicago, IL 60605-2496
(312) 922 9410
Web site: http://fieldmuseum.org
The Field Museum provides the opportunity to explore an ancient Egyptian tomb. Visitors can view mummies, hieroglyphs, and more.

Metropolitan Museum of Art
1000 Fifth Avenue
New York, NY 10028-0198
(212) 535-7710
Web site: http://www.metmuseum.org
This museum's outstanding collection of ancient Egyptian
   art numbers about twenty-six thousand objects.

Rosicrucian Egyptian Museum & Planetarium
1660 Park Avenue
San Jose, CA 95191
(408) 947-3635
Web site: http://www.egyptianmuseum.org
The Rosicrucian Egyptian Museum & Planetarium houses
   the largest collection of Egyptian artifacts on exhibit in
   western North America.

Society for the Study of Egyptian Antiquities
P.O. Box 19004 Walmer
360A Bloor Street W
Toronto, ON M5S 3C9
Canada
(647) 520-4339
Web site: http://www.thessea.org
The Society for the Study of Egyptian Antiquities has chap-
   ters in four Canadian cities. It was founded to promote
   interest and enthusiasm in Egyptology.

Theban Mapping Project
The American University in Cairo
113 Sharia Kasr El Aini
P.O. Box 2511
Cairo, Egypt
Web site: http://www.thebanmappingproject.com
This organization is dedicated to preserving the remnants
    of the ancient world in Thebes in Egypt.

Web Sites

Due to the changing nature of Internet links, Rosen Publishing
has developed an online list of Web sites related to the subject
of this book. This site is updated regularly. Please use this link
to access the list:

http://www.rosenlinks.com/EAC/Egypt

FOR FURTHER READING

Bancroft-Hunt, Norman. *Living in Ancient Egypt* (Living in the Ancient World). New York, NY: Chelsea House Publishers, 2009.

Booth, Charlotte. *The Curse of the Mummy: And Other Mysteries of Ancient Egypt*. Oxford, England: Oneworld, 2009.

Bramwell, Neil D. *Discover Ancient Egypt* (Discover Ancient Civilizations). Berkeley Heights, NJ: Enslow Publishers, 2014.

Fitzgerald, Stephanie. *Ramses II: Egyptian Pharoah, Warrior, and Builder* (Signature Lives). Minneapolis, MN: CompassPoint Books, 2009.

Kallen, Stuart A. *Ancient Egypt* (Understanding World History). San Diego, CA: ReferencePoint Press, 2012.

Kerrigan, Michael. *Egyptians* (Ancients in Their Own Words). New York, NY: Marshall Cavendish Benchmark, 2011.

Mertz, Barbara. *Red Land, Black Land: Daily Life in Ancient Egypt*. New York, NY: Harper, 2009.

Mertz, Barbara. *Temples, Tombs, & Hieroglyphs: A Popular History of Ancient Egypt*. New York, NY: William Morrow, 2007.

Mueller, Steven. *The Pharaohs of Ancient Egypt*. Brookfield, IL: Waldmann Press, 2009.

Ollhoff, Jim. *Egyptian Mythology* (World of Mythology). Edina, MN: ABDO Publishing, 2011.

Pemberton, Delia. *The Civilization of Ancient Egypt* (Illustrated History of the Ancient World). New York, NY: Rosen Publishing, 2013.

Preston, Diana. *Cleopatra and Antony: Power, Love, and Politics in the Ancient World*. New York, NY: Walker Publishing, 2009.

Romer, John. *The Great Pyramid: Ancient Egypt Revisited.* New York, NY: Cambridge University Press, 2007.

Romer, John. *A History of Ancient Egypt from the First Farmers to the Great Pyramid.* New York, NY: Thomas Dunne Books, 2013.

Sheafer, Silvia Anne. *Ramses the Great* (Ancient World Leaders). New York, NY: Chelsea House, 2009.

Sims, Lesley, and Emma Dodd. *Ancient Egypt* (Visitor's Guides). London, England: Usborne Publishing, 2009.

Snedden, Robert. *Ancient Egypt* (Technology in Times Past). Mankato, MN: Smart Apple Media, 2009.

Teeter, Emily, and Janet H. Johnson. *The Life of Meresamun: A Temple Singer in Ancient Egypt.* Chicago, IL: Oriental Institute of the University of Chicago, 2009.

Thomas, J. S. *The Real History of Ancient Egypt.* Victoria, BC: Trafford Publishing, 2009.

Tignor, Robert L. *Egypt: A Short History.* Princeton, NJ: Princeton University Press, 2011.

INDEX

About the Author

Therese Shea, an editor and former educator, has written more than one hundred fifty books on a variety of subjects, including American and world history. She holds degrees from Providence College and the State University of New York at Buffalo. The author resides in Atlanta, Georgia, with her husband, Mark.

Photo Credits

Cover Kenneth Garrett/National Geographic Image Collection/Getty Images; cover (background), p. 1 Triff/Shutterstock.com; p. 5 Jacques Descloitres, MODIS Rapid Response Team, NASA/GSFC; p. 9 Prasit Chansareekorn/Flickr Vision/Getty Images; p. 11 The Sydney Morning Herald/Fairfax Media/Getty Images; p. 14 DEA/A. Dagli Orti/De Agostini/Getty Images; pp. 16, 21 AFP/Getty Images; p. 22 Patrick Landmann/Getty Images; pp. 24–25 The Bridgeman Art Library/Getty Images; p. 27 Raphael Gaillarde/Gamma-Rapho/Getty Images; p. 29 Gerard Sioen/Gamma-Rapho/Getty Images; p. 31 pidjoe/E+/Getty Images; p. 35 DEA/G. Dagli Orti/De Agostini/Getty Images; p. 38 DEA Picture Library/Getty Images; p. 42 Werner Forman/Universal Images Group/Getty Images; p. 45 Reuters/Landov; p. 46 © AP Images; p. 50 Phillip Hayson/Photolibrary/Getty Images; back cover daulon /Shutterstock.com; cover, back cover, and interior pages graphic elements R-studio/Shutterstock.com (gold texture), brem stocker /Shutterstock.com (compass icon), Konyayeva/Shutterstock.com (banner pattern).

Designer: Michael Moy; Editor: Andrea Sclarow Paskoff; Photo Researcher: Amy Feinberg